ESSAY

ON THE

HISTORY AND GROWTH

OF THE

OF PHILADELPHIA,

AND ON ITS

CAPABILITIES FOR FUTURE USEFULNESS.

Published by Order of the Board of Managers.

PHILADELPHIA:
JAS. B. RODGERS, PRINTER, 52 & 54 NORTH SIXTH ST.
1867.

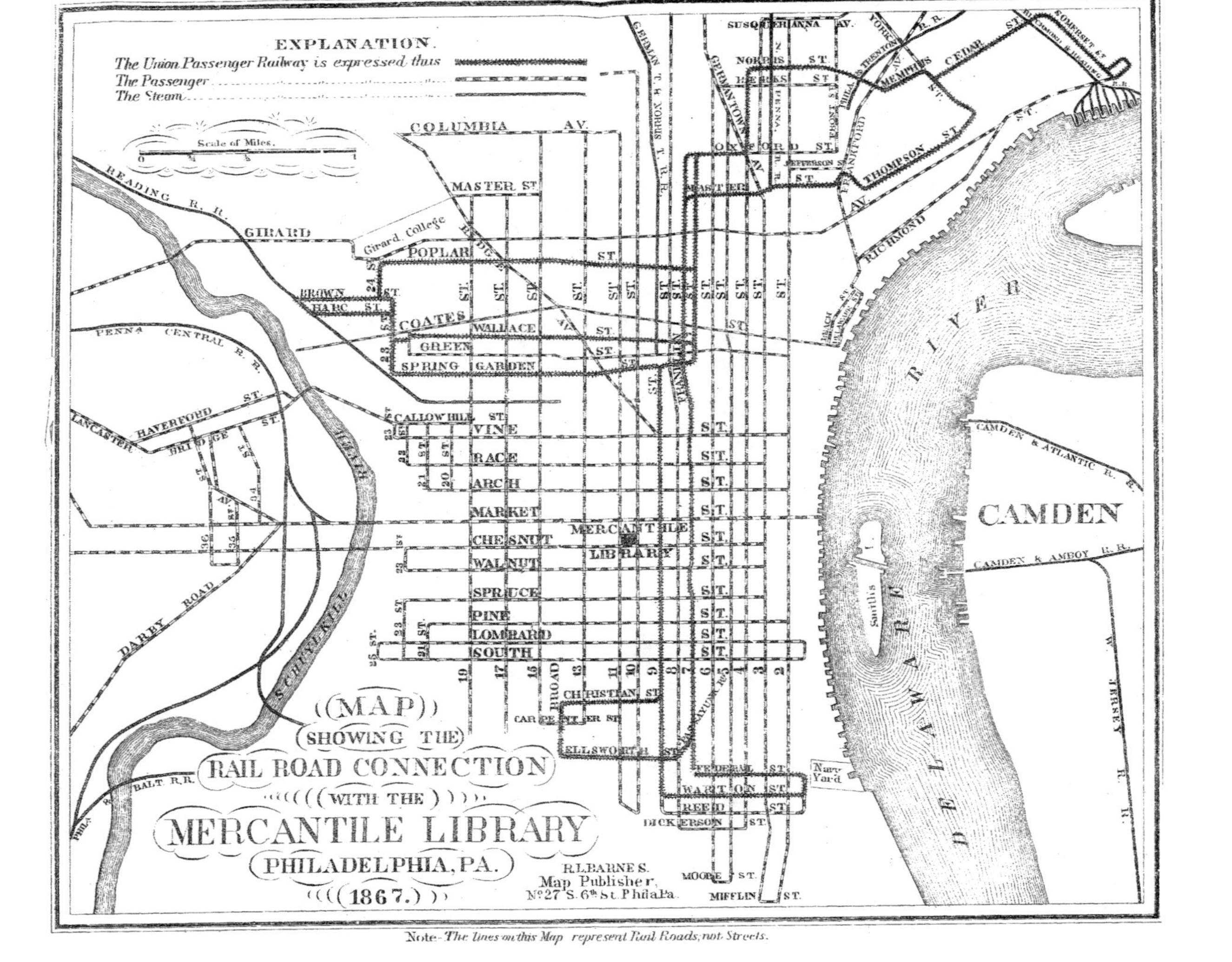

Note- *The lines on this Map represent Rail Roads, not Streets.*

ESSAY

ON THE

HISTORY AND GROWTH

OF THE

MERCANTILE LIBRARY CO.

OF PHILADELPHIA,

AND ON ITS

CAPABILITIES FOR FUTURE USEFULNESS.

PUBLISHED BY ORDER OF THE BOARD OF MANAGERS.

PHILADELPHIA:
JAS. B. RODGERS, PRINTER, 52 & 54 NORTH SIXTH STREET.
1867.

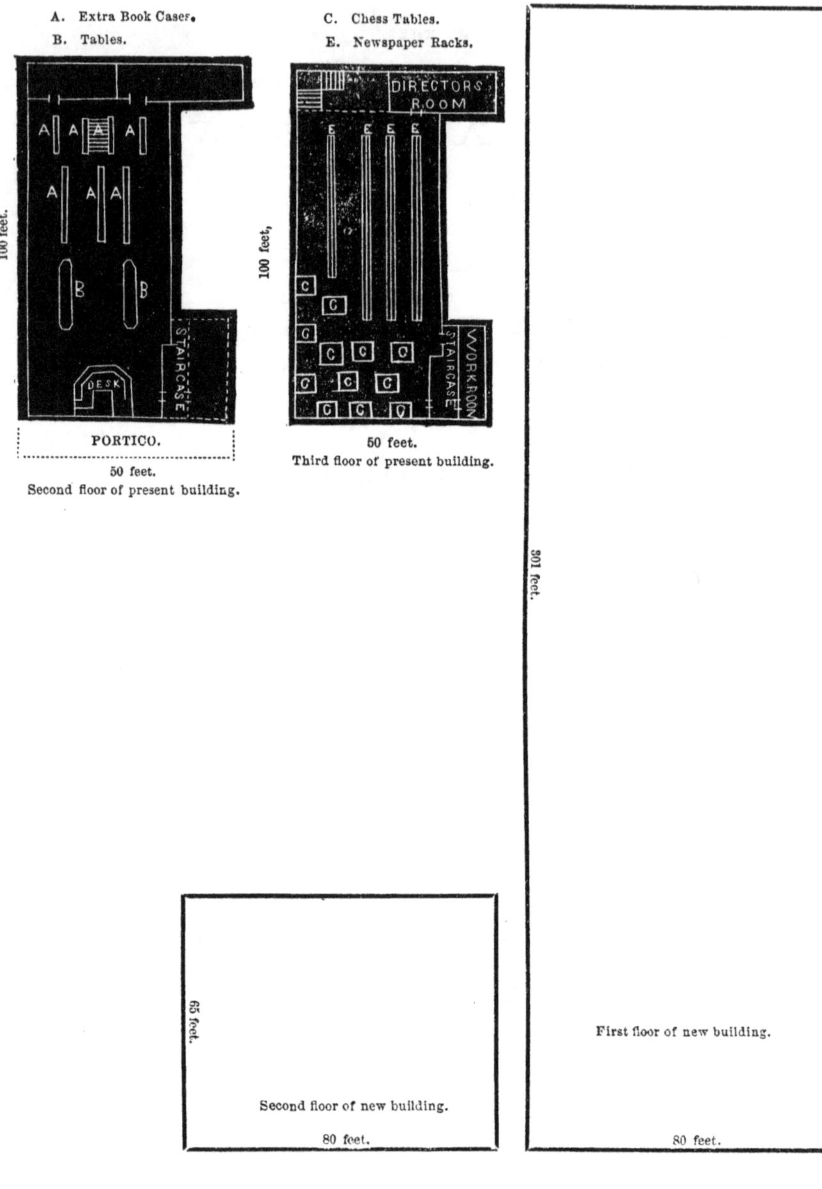

Second floor of present building.

Third floor of present building.

Second floor of new building.

First floor of new building.

AN ESSAY

ON THE HISTORY AND GROWTH OF THE MERCANTILE LIBRARY COMPANY OF PHILADELPHIA.

It is not often that greater results have grown from small beginnings than those which have come from the founding of the New York Mercantile Library in 1820, and that of Philadelphia, one year later.

These were followed in the next decade by like institutions in Baltimore, Buffalo and Cincinnati, and have been the patterns upon which all the popular or free libraries of the Union have been modeled.

The seed dropped in fruitful soil, and nurtured by careful hands; the leaven hidden in a mass, capable of being improved by it, have grown up, and spread their power into a continually widening influence.

The Mercantile Library of our city was of very humble origin, but its birth was presided over by men who were then the foremost in commercial activity and influence, and who have left behind them in accumulated fortunes, or in honored families, or remembered worth, monuments of excellence that should guide those who would now emulate their careers.

On November 10th, 1821, at the Masonic Hall, was held the first meeting to deliberate upon the foundation of a "Mercantile Library Association;" from it emanated a public notice inviting "merchants, merchants' clerks and others" to meet at the Mayor's Office, on the 17th, to consider the same subject.

Here Robert Waln, Robert Ralston, Joseph P. Norris, Zaccheus Collins, Bernard Dahlgren, John Roberts, Joseph H. Dulles, William H. Jones and William E. Bowen, were appointed a committee to draft a Constitution.

On the 1st of December, the Constitution was adopted by an adjourned meeting, and a committee of fifteen was appointed to procure subscribers to it, with instructions to give public notice of an election for Directors whenever one hundred were obtained.

Three hundred enrolled themselves, and on the 10th of January, 1822, an election was held at the Merchants' Coffee House, in Second Street, near

Walnut, (now included in the brown stone building on the N. W. cor. of 2d and Walnut,) where the following gentlemen were chosen

DIRECTORS.

JOSEPH P. NORRIS,	WILLIAM L. HODGE,
ROBERT WALN,	CALEB NEWBOLD, JR.,
LANGDON CHEVES,	WILLIAM H. JONES,
BERNARD DAHLGREN,	WILLIAM E. BOWEN,
THOMAS BIDDLE,	JOHN M. ATWOOD,
WILLIAM CHALONER,	NICHOLAS THOURON,

WILLIAM M. WALMSLEY.

JOSEPH H. DULLES, *Treasurer.*

Let us dwell a moment upon the names of these gentlemen.

Of these, four were bankers; Mr. Norris being the President of the Bank of Penna.; Mr. Cheves, a South Carolinian, President of the Bank of the United States; Mr. Biddle a private banker and broker of large fortune, and Mr. Walmsley of the same profession. Mr. Bowen was afterwards connected with, and became the resident Philadelphia partner of, the House of Brown Bros., which, through its connections in Liverpool, New York, Baltimore and New Orleans, has acquired a celebrity, both European and American. Mr. Chaloner was the senior partner of Chaloner & Henry; Mr. J. S. Henry being the father of Alexander Henry, late Mayor of the city. He and Mr. Thouron were both engaged in the wholesale dry goods business; Mr. Thouron being a French importer. William H. Jones was a famous auction crier, and Bernard Dahlgren was an accountant and book-keeper in a large commercial establishment; both are remembered as men of mental power and cultivation. Mr. Dahlgren was a Swede, and father of the present Admiral. Mr. Newbold, a man of an ardent temperament, was at one period of his life engaged in mercantile pursuits. For many years he had charge of the Delaware and Chesapeake Canal; first as Superintendent, and afterwards as President.

Mr. Hodge, Mr. Atwood and Mr. Dulles are the only survivors of the original Board. Of their personal merits it is, therefore, not now proper to speak. But a grateful appreciation of their exertions should induce the record, that to the care, assiduity and zeal of Messrs. Atwood, Dulles & Bowen the Mercantile Library of Philadelphia owes its rise and a large measure of its early success.

By the gentlemen just recounted Mr. Waln was chosen President of the Board. His great-grandfather was one of the "Friends" who came over with William Penn. He inherited a handsome estate, and became one of the most prominent merchants of the city, being engaged in the West India and English shipping business, and for many years in the East India and China trade.

He was also one of the earliest manufacturers of the country, having erected a cotton factory at Trenton in 1812, and engaged in Iron Works at Phœnixville. He became a leading advocate of the doctrine of protection.

Mr. Waln for some years served in the State Legislature, and was elected to Congress in 1798. Honest, manly, generous, and courteous, he brought to this youthful enterprise the countenance of a name for years distinguished by ability and worth.

The second-story rooms of Robt. Winebrenner's store, No. 100 Chestnut Street, having been leased for a rent of $150, the Library was opened to its members on the 5th of March.

Having found a location, a librarian was advertised for. The salary of this officer being fixed at $100 per annum, bonds were required of him for $400. The duty was assigned him of opening the rooms from 6 to 10, P. M., every evening, and of attending to the business of the Library. Forty-one applicants were found ready to accept these responsibilities and emoluments.

The Mercantile Library, as its name implies, was not originally a company, but an "Association." It was not composed of shareholders, having certificates of stock, but of members paying initiation fees and semi-annual contributions. The former being $3.00 each; the latter, $1. It elected a Treasurer, but no President or other general officer. The first meeting of the Directors was held January 14th, 1822, at the counting-house of A. Henry & Co. Mr. Waln was made President of the Board, and Mr. Bowen, Secretary.

The duty of selecting and purchasing books was delegated to a committee of five, three of whom, Messrs. Atwood, Dulles and Walmsley, served up to the year 1838, and from 1829 to 1838 without colleagues.

During the year 1822, nine hundred dollars were appropriated to it. And if the entry, six times repeated this year, upon the Directors' minute-book, "no quorum present at the monthly meetings," be any indication of the attention of the Board at other times, the further care and charge of the Library must have fallen mainly upon the purchasing committee.

It is interesting to note, as an indication of the foreign commerce of Philadelphia in the early years of this century, that in December, 1822, the masters and officers of vessels were invited to visit the Library Rooms; and that four years later a committee was appointed to wait on the captains in port, for the sake of procuring from them articles of curiosity, and to invite them to the rooms, and make a reception for the solicited gifts.

The Library grew rather slowly in books. In its third year fifteen hundred were upon its shelves. Three hundred and forty of these were deposited with it by its friends. Nor was its increase in membership more successful. It had begun with over three hundred members, and up to its third year its rolls had contained but few over three hundred and eighty. From these various resignations occurred, and even "among those punctual in the payment of their dues, a general apathy existed." So that "of all the dues for 1824, but about $100 were collected." Two remedies were proposed for this disheartening condition: That the Library should be rendered more attractive by taking newspapers, and that members of the Board should assist the Treasurer in urging upon subscribers the payment of dues. The first recommendation resulted, during the next year, in taking three Philadelphia and two New York dailies,—the nucleus of the great newspaper and periodical department of the Library as it now exists. The necessity of the second was superseded by a very important change in the Constitution of the Library, which was effected in 1826, by turning it from an "Association" of subscribers into an incorporated Company of stockholders.

A charter was obtained; the property of the Association valued, and divided into three hundred shares of ten dollars each, subject to an annual "due" of one dollar. In 1831 this payment was raised to two dollars, and in 1863 to three dollars, as was required to supply more completely the wants of the members. This change to a stock basis has had very important advantages. It confers upon the Company control of its revenues, by enabling it to forfeit the stock of delinquents in payment of dues, and to the stockholder it gives an augmented interest in the Library, arising from a sense of the personal attachment of his ownership in it, as well as a dislike to be delinquent in the discharge of his annual pecuniary obligation.

This change, however desirable, was not very rapidly effected. There are records of seventy-seven stockholders having been acquired in 1826, one hundred and thirty in the next year, and it is stated in the report of 1828, that there were two hundred and eighty-seven stockholders and sixty subscribers; in all, three hundred and forty-seven members, and this is the first exact statement that can be found of the numbers belonging to the Library.

But from the first, the resolution to form a Stock Company seems to have inspired new vigor, and complaints of languishment were afterward seldom heard.

In 1826 the Library was removed to the second story of the N. W. corner of Fifth and Chestnut Streets.

Here, in January of the next year, the Board congratulates itself upon the "highly prosperous condition," which so continues, that in October, for the sake of "additional conveniences," it is forced to a removal to the second-story rooms of the Sunday-school Union Building, on the south side of Chestnut, above Sixth, where are now the stores, west of the new *Ledger* Building.

Upon the modest furniture and equipment of these rooms was expended $150, including the price of "two beautiful hanging lamps," whose effectual "illumination" is spoken of in glowing terms by the committee of superintendence.

But other evidence of progress is given, more substantial than the glow of astral lamp, or even of the enthusiasm of a committee, by the investment of five hundred dollars of surplus funds in the Bonds of the Delaware & Chesapeake Canal, in March, 1828, and by the publication, near the close of the year, of an edition of five hundred catalogues.

Between the years 1828 and 1835, several courses of lectures were delivered under the auspices of this Institution. Their titles (so far as known) show that they were intended to impart information and solid instruction on subjects of importance to business men. The well-known names of their authors guarantee their excellence.

In 1837–8 began a series of brilliant discourses, which for several years were delivered by eminent public men brought from all parts of the country by the joint care of the Mercantile Library and the Athenian Institute. These, delivered to crowded audiences in the Musical Fund Hall, were marked events in city life. One of these, given in 1839 by John Sergeant, on Mercantile Character, so fully breathes the spirit of that pure heart and noble mind, that we cannot avoid calling attention to the fact of its existence in the Library in print.

For some unexplained reasons the course of 1856 resulted in a loss of nearly $800, and none have since been given.

A circumstance that occurred in February, 1827, may form a fitting introduction to some remarks upon the character of the literature stored in and being acquired by the Library. At that time a Society newly established in this city for the defence of a powerful religious organization against "calumny and abuse," having delivered at the Library, free of expense, a miscellany published in its support, it was "resolved that no newspaper or periodical publication professingly designed to advance the interests of any particular religious sect be admitted into the Library."

Until a few years ago, this rule was strictly adhered to. It was not that exclusion was sought for against religious doctrinal views, but that non-intervention in current polemics was the position desired. No hostile attitude was ever assumed against any form of earnest thought. The standard writers of every religion or denomination; the expounders of each great system of faith and feeling on which the human mind has been moulded; the early Christian fathers, Luther, Cranmer, Calvin, Milton, Barclay, Bolingbroke, Hume, Paine, Voltaire, the Talmud, the Koran, Mœhler, Balmes, Spaulding or Kendrick, and many others are upon our shelves.

About three years ago, the application of the rule restricting religious periodicals was relaxed, and now the *Church Review*, the *Dublin Review*, the *Independent*, the *Episcopalian*, the weeklies of the "Friends," the *Universe*, the *Occident*, and several others of the same sort, without any jangling or jarring, lie peacefully side by side upon the broad tables of our literary emporium.

From the grave we would turn to the lighter forms of literature, and say a few words upon that great feature of every popular Library—the Novel department—endeavoring to state the simple facts concerning it. This is the chief attraction to the greater number of those who use such a Library as the Mercantile. About two-thirds of the emissions of books are of Novels. In number, they are about one-sixth of the whole collection, and they cost annually one-tenth of the whole money spent in reading matter. These figures are in part conjectural. In 1858 a record was kept of the emission of books by classes, when sixty per cent. of the whole was found to be of Novels. The proportion has since increased, a larger stock of them having been bought. Oversight is exercised in their selection, so as to insure that any which could be properly classed among "immoral or pernicious works," shall be rejected. And it is believed that few or none of such obtain admittance. If any such are discovered, they are removed. Further than this, the right of censorship is not exercised, excepting that in selecting those upon which the money appropriated to novels shall be spent, those of the highest grade and most nearly classic may be chosen.

This end being guarded, enough is bought of each kind to supply the IMPORTUNATE demand. More is done to satisfy the calls for new works on their first appearance, than is supposed by many. As illustrations of the practice in this matter: the Library is now furnished with 20 to 40 of each of Dickens, 20 to 30 of Bayard Taylor, and 40 of each of Miss Muhlbach's ten books, the novels now running.

This system of duplication is carried out in all standard works much sought for. For example, of Macaulay there are 40 vols ; of Prescott, 60 ; of Bancroft, 25 ; of Hume, 25 ; and of Irving, 60. In a word, it is not sought to legislate, in matters grave or gay, for or against wants or desires ; but to use the means at command to the best advantage in supplying the best of these desires.

But the narrative should not be further interrupted by this digression. The history of the Institution has been briefly traced for the first seven years ; its early struggles have been exhibited ; the principles that governed its life and growth have been shown. It now began to exhibit signs of expansion ; feeble at first, but constant. Two hundred additional shares were authorized by the Annual Meeting of 1829, which proved enough to supply the market for several years.

In 1831 a discussion seems to have arisen as to whether it were better policy to procure funds to meet the wants of the stockholders by sales of further shares ; or limiting the shares to the number already authorized, to acquire money by augmenting the dues to two dollars. After a twelve months' debate, the latter plan was adopted. Experience has demonstrated that to have accepted the more expansive one also, had been wiser. In 1835 or 1836, which it is not certainly known, the necessity of meeting the demand for stock brought this about. And from this time the era of restriction in the sales of stock ceased, and all wants were supplied as they arose.

The active, buoyant life of the Institution now began. With a few slight fluctuations, annual increase, not rapid, but steady, in members, books owned, bought and loaned, receipts and expeditures, marks its history for the next thirty years.

A youth of noble principles, in the first flushings of manly vigor, is filled with generous enthusiasm and impulse ; his after years are fruitful of action and earnest deeds. In like manner, the Reports of the Library Company in the first years of strength, are filled with sentiment. Details of business occupy the late years.

A few quotations will show the animus which prevailed. The Report of January, 1843, speaking of the object of the Company, says :

"A great object of the formation of this Library Company, was the elevation of the standard of mercantile character; its design was to furnish the "young men of business not only with innocent amusement, but to supply "them with motives to intellectual exertion and moral improvement; to im- "press them with a sense of their opportunities and responsibilities, and that "in seeking to be successful merchants, they ought also to be men—men, "with views of duty beyond the limits of their business, and that the basis of "the mercantile character ought to be the manly character." And the same report uses words of warning and encouragement after a period similar in its commercial features to that we are now passing through.

"It has been a frequent observation of late, that the disorders and depression "which have restrained the action of commerce, impaired the fortunes of many, "and almost paralyzed the energies of men of business, have also impressed "the minds of some with the lesson, that the slow but sure avails of perse- "vering industry is a more certain means for the attainment of character and "competency, than the fruits of the insanity of speculation, which would drive "to opulence with rail-road velocity, and with its rapid alternations of gain "and loss, leave its votaries incapable of exerting the power of self-culture. "The delusion of speculation has departed, but the present repose of the "elements of business activity cannot always continue; the dormant spirit of "commercial enterprise will revive; trade will again attract to its pursuit the "energies of men, and the experience of the past will be useless unless its "warnings be transplanted to the future."

The report of January, 1846, admonishes the youthful members thus:

"We trust that it will not be considered irrelevant to the duties of the "Board if this occasion is used to remind the youthful members of the Asso- "ciation, that to them this Institution may prove to be an inestimable bless- "ing if they avail themselves of the aids here afforded for the acquisition of "knowledge and the cultivation of moral worth. You have the facilities, and "your period of life furnishes time for mental cultivation. Hereafter, with "the cares and duties of middle or advanced age pressing on you, if you have "been indifferent to your early advantages, you will discover that neglected "means of improvement never return, but that regretful memory will recall "precious hours of leisure misapplied, and opportunities of good lost forever.

"Well directed reading and thought will assist to form close and accurate "observations of life and character, and he will be best qualified for the busi- "ness of the world, who has just conceptions of the duties of his position, "and the requisite ability for meeting them."

After the Mexican War and the gold discoveries, in prospect of the trade of California and of the Pacific Ocean, and of the facilities of rail and steamer now being extended towards them, the report of 1849 says:

"Regarding carefully the important transactions of the eventful period in "which we live, and impressed by the magnitude of the results, as influencing "not only the present, but all future time, the young merchant and the clerk "will perceive the importance of mental culture, and that of a high character. "Intelligence will promote success. By intelligence we mean not only a "technical knowledge of the details of commercial business, but general and "accurate information of the social and political condition of the world; the "habits and wants of the people of its several divisions; their systems of "trade and finance, all those facts and principles which govern their inter- "course with nations and individuals.

"Correct habits of thought will render knowledge available for useful and "profitable purposes. It is the design of the Mercantile Library to encourage "these habits and impart this information."

The words of worthy Boards of by-gone days should be commended to attention. And with confidence in the efficacy of its teachings, the Board enters the region of prophecy; the following prediction is made:

"The Board may confidently predict, that in future times the Philadelphia "merchants who shall stand pre-eminent in society for unwavering rectitude, "refined intelligence, just liberality, and social and business prosperity, will "be found among those who passed the precious evenings of their youth "within the treasure-lined walls of the MERCANTILE LIBRARY HALL."

Those disposed to learn the history of the Institution from 1830 to 1860, will find the major details in the tabular statement. A few minor points, less important than curious, may be noted here.

In 1832, Henry D. Gilpin, chairman of the committee of arrangements for the great civic procession on the Centennial Anniversary of Washington's birth, invited the members to walk in the procession. The invitation, in consequence of "the members generally belonging to other societies or professions," was declined. The Library, however, was closed in honor of the occasion. It was also closed in August of the same year, at 8 P. M., on account of the prevalence of cholera.

In June, 1837, is found the following minute: "The *Knickerbocker* and the *Public Ledger* having become *popular*, it has been suggested that the Library should subscribe for them. [Signed] J. COX, *Librarian*."

In 1839 died Wm. Mason Walmsley, from its foundation to within a year of his death, a member of the Board, and a faithful worker for the Mercantile Library. He was a single man, and is remembered for gentle bearing, and cultivated, refined character.

Thomas P. Cope, for thirty-one years President of the Library, died in 1854, in his eighty-fourth year. He, like Robert Waln, was a Quaker. Removing from Lancaster County in 1786, he began, four years later, a business career, which has passed into the commercial history of Philadelphia. Some offices of political trust were offered to and accepted by him, and others declined.

In the ways of benevolence his path was most crowned with usefulness. As "Manager of the Almshouse," and the "Pennsylvania Hospital;" as "Guardian of the Poor," and as one who tarried to combat, and suffered from the plague of, yellow fever, which desolated the city in 1793, and again in 1797, should Mr. Cope's name be endeared to the hearts of the people. The kindliness of his nature, his genial warmth and humor, his enterprise, guarded by a wise caution, his sagacity, and the many other noble qualities of his character, dwell in the memory of a large circle of his friends.

In 1855 John Faussett died. He had served the Company four years as Director, and subsequently, for twenty-five years, as its Treasurer, having, from ill health, resigned this position the year before his death. The Institution, which he faithfully labored to support, has honored him by placing his portrait upon its walls by the side of its early President.

In the period under notice, viz: from 1830–60, the most remarkable event was the erection of the graceful structure in which the Library is now located.

After three changes, in the year 1835, the residence of the Library was fixed in the 2nd story of the house west of the Custom House, where is now the U. S. Post Office, and which was long the resort of the fashion and elegance of the town in the days of Lyon J. Levy & Co.

The property changed owners in 1843. The Library was warned out.

In this emergency it was determined to carry out a design that had long been entertained:—The Library should be no longer an outcast and an emigrant, it should possess a handsome hall, a local habitation of its own. The lot 100 x 36 feet, on the corner of Fifth and Library Streets, was bought, on *condition that funds could be procured to complete the project.*

The annual meeting of January 9th, 1844, approved the purchase provided the funds could be raised by the *first day of the February following.* Thirty gentlemen were appointed to aid the Directors in procuring subscriptions. "In a very few days" upwards of fourteen-thousand dollars were subscribed "by the members and the public." A building fund of thirty-four hundred dollars had been already laid by, chiefly from the profits of lectures. Feeling that these sums would sustain the enterprise, the Directors closed the contract for the lot, (the heirs of Dr. James Gallager being the owners,) and subsequently added to it, a strip fourteen feet wide, purchased of the Philadelphia Dispensary. Fifty-feet by one hundred, thus became the graceful proportions of the parallelogram on which the simple and chaste Grecian edifice is placed.

Its entire cost was $44,199. In its erection a debt was incurred of $22,969.

In July 1845, the books were removed to it. One of the original Board still served as director. Others and many early friends were alive to exult in its prosperity. And in remembering the one 2nd story room of 1822,—hired at a meagre rent—the half-paid librarian,—the book committee economizing funds by rummaging the stores of second-hand dealers; in recollection of the early struggle, the toil of nearly a fourth part of a century—these first and fast friends, upon the evening when luminous with gas-light, and in elegance of fresh polish, it was opened to public inspection, must have regarded their work with a proud thankfulness, that their labors had been blessed with so noble a consummation.

At the foundation of the Library, its benefits, open to all, were intended mainly for merchants and their clerks. It is probable that men of no other avocation would, for their own sakes, have arranged a collection which would have become so suited to popular tastes. It is the habit of the business mind to understand the wants of the general community, and to supply them; it may be for this reason that the Mercantile Libraries have in most of our cities, become the leading distributors of reading matter to the public. This has been evidently the case with ours, during the past nine years. A small effort will now enable it to extend its influences much more widely among all classes, and into every section of the city.

Since 1859, foreign books have been regularly ordered through a special agent resident in London. The yearly importations comprise several hundred volumes of choice and unique publications, also, desirable or rare selections from the catalogues of large second-hand dealers.

One of the most pleasing offices of the Company has been to serve, during 1862, as distributor of donations of reading matter sent to it, by the charitable, for the use of army hospitals of the city. Six thousand five hundred articles, of reading matter, aided in soothing the hours of convalescence of the wounded or sickened soldier.

The proportion of the membership of the Library, to the population of the city, has been in constantly increasing ratio. For every ten thousand inhabitants, in 1830, there were 27 members; in 1840, 29; in 1850, 36; in 1860, 43; and in 1866, it was 80 to the ten thousand. This process has been going on at the same time with the removal of dwellings and of population from the vicinity of the Library.

In 1864, the shares of stock were duplicated; 3100 (in round numbers) were issued. The market price of the shares was lessened for a few months but is now nearly the same as before duplication.

These facts show not only, an ever growing appreciation of the advantages of the Library, but, indicate that a large number of shares could be absorbed in a short period. An increase of only 39 members last year, and in this year of but few more, shows that the limit of the power of the Library to serve the public in its present condition has been reached, as it was in the three years preceding the purchase of its present site in 1844.

An infusion of new strength is needed to support even its life; for growth is the law of life; when enthusiasm ceases, torpor comes.

Could there be now, as in 1844, a plan perfected by which the 6,200 members of this year, could have as ample room as the 900 of that, can it be doubted that equally important results would follow?

It is not well to anticipate too greatly. But it is reasonable to suppose, that the Library would enjoy a revenue of $40,000, and distribute its blessings to 12,000 members within ten years. Last year the amount spent in reading matter, and laid by in building fund is 60 per cent. of the gross receipts. At this rate there could be spent in reading matter $24,000 which would purchase besides news-papers and periodicals, 15,300 volumes at the average cost of books in 1866, viz: $1.70. This would be an annual increase greater than the whole Library in 1857,—the 35th year of its existence. And in the case supposed, of a doubling of its members, and more than doubling its advantages, the books loaned would not be less than 400,000 to 500,000 volumes.

A duplication of membership in ten years, and an increase of population of the city, at the rate it has augmented in the last seven years, would make the proportion of the former to the latter, 107 in every ten thousand.

A glance at the table on the opposite page, giving the like ratios for other cities, will make it evident that this is not an extravagant calculation.

COMPARATIVE STATISTICS OF POPULAR LIBRARIES.

NAME OF LIBRARY.	When Founded.	No. Members in 1866.	No. Volumes in 1866.	Volumes loaned in 1866.	Newspapers, etc. on file 1866.	Cost of Membership.	Value of Building, or Rent of Rooms.	Est. Population, City, 1866.	Number of Members to every 10,000 inhabitants.	N. B.—In the column of Cost of Membership, the upper number is the amount of Initiation fee, or par value of Stock expressed in dollars. The lower, the corresponding Annual payment.
Philadelphia M. L. Co.	1821	6,167	40,000 est.	177,003 est.	300	$\frac{10}{3}$ or $\frac{0}{5}$		766,232	80	
Merc. L. of Baltimore	1839	1,357	20,559	33,925	63	* $\frac{0}{5}$ or † $\frac{2}{3}$	‡ $35,000 bef. war.	300,000 in '65	44	‡ Occupy first floor of three, rent free. * Anybody. † Clerks.
Young Men's Ass., Albany	1833	* 2,303	10,616	30,000		† $\frac{0}{2}$	R. $1,250	62,613	367	† Lecture Tickets, $3.00 extra. * March, '67.
New York M. L. Ass.	1820	10,000	90,000	231,000	400	$\frac{0}{5}$ or $\frac{1}{3}$	$350,000 cost	1,000,000 inc. Roxb	100	
Boston Athenæum	1807	825	100,000		194		$250,000	230,000		
Wilmington Library	1787	533	7,255	26,208	55	* $\frac{1}{4}$		30,000 '67 ?	153	* Including Lectures.
Young Men's Mer. Ass., Buffalo,	1835	2,800	13,000	37,130	65	$\frac{1}{3}$	$150,000 orig. cost	140,000	200	
Free Pub. L. of Worcester	1859		20,000	66,000	97	00	$30,000	40,000		
Free Pub. L. of New Bedford	1852		20,000	35,405	35	00	$44,000	22,000		

Just such a plan is being prosecuted. What is needed to perfect it?

The Company has bought the Franklin Market House, in Tenth Street, above Chestnut. It has an area of 24,080 feet; two rooms now occupied have 8,000; as one floor only was employed in 1845, the proportion between the two houses is the same as between the members then and now, viz:—1 and 6.

The undertaking therefore is not more in advance of the wants of this day than was that of 1844. The 10th street house is surrounded by passenger railways. It is in the centre of their system, as a look at the map will show, equidistant from League Island and Kensington. By them it can be reached from the most remote part of the city within thirty minutes. The machinist of Kensington, the ship builder at League Island, the weaver and spinner from Fairmount, can at pleasure visit it after the labor of the day, and return home at an early hour for the night's repose.

What is needed to secure this prize? Let us see.

Its cost price is, ...	$126,000.		
Upon which there is a ground rent,	50,000.		
Leaving cash to be paid, . .	$ 76,000.		
To warm, light, floor, partition, renovate, beautify and furnish (estimate by Fraser), will cost, . . .	76,000.		
Leaving to complete it all, . .			$152,000
How is this to be raised?			
There is a building fund of		$30,000,	
Assessed value of the present Library Building, ...	$ 80,000.		
Mortgage upon it, . . .	7,000.		
		73,000.	
			103,000
There is therefore needed, ...			$49,000

This is the lowest sum which will confer upon the Library a house worthy of it, and even this under an incumbrance of $50,000. Ninety-nine Thousand, or the round sum of One Hundred Thousand Dollars is essential to insure to Philadelphia a popular Library, commensurate with the wants of the city, without the oppression of debt upon it.

From whence is this to come?

For the second time only in its history, the Library now appeals for aid. Its revenues have sufficed to supply its collections of literature, and to earn a portion of the capital expended in real estate. Nothing has been received as donations save the four legacies, incorporated in the four book funds, and the contributions towards the present building in 1844. A donation from S. Morris Waln this year is the only exception to this remark. These donations were repaid in stock or in scrip, which has yielded a large per cent. of cost to the subscribers. The savings from its current receipts which have been applied to erecting its building, and paying off incumbrances against it, have exceeded the amount secured from subscriptions for the same end.

A generous public will not fail to assist those so willing to help themselves.

Most of the thousands who belong to the Library are young men and women, whose means allow them to own a single share, or pay an annual subscription, but are not ample enough to enable them to donate to it or to hold its scrip largely. Some are of advanced wealth and position, having characters formed from such influences as the Library presents.

To these and to the general public, has this appeal been set forth; and in behalf of the thousands who belong, and should be attracted to the Mercantile Library,—has this narrative been written.

Reader are you poor? Buy a share of stock, that with this investment the wealth of knowledge may be secure to you? Are you TOO poor for this? Then subscribe yearly, and labor hard to earn and save the money to meet it.

Are you rich? Why do you possess your wealth—only to wrap yourself in fine raiment and live delicately? No; it is to aid your fellow-man in noble ways! Aid him, then, by giving from your store to rear this temple of learning. Or if you wish not to give, buy its stock, and hold it until your poorer brother will re-buy it of you. You would, of your means, save him from starving; having saved him, will not you place the bread of knowledge in his reach? "Many a man lives a burden to the earth; but a good book is the precious life-blood of a master-spirit imbalmed and treasured up on purpose for a life beyond life." Will you shut out any one from this life? No.

"I deny not, but that it is of greatest concernment in the Church and Commonwealth, to have a vigilant eye how books demean themselves as well as men; and thereafter to confine, imprison, and do sharpest justice on them as malefactors; for books are not absolutely dead things, but do contain a progeny of life in them to be as active as that soul was whose progeny they are; nay, they do preserve as in a vial the purest efficacy and extraction of that living intellect that bred them. I know they are as lively, and as vigorously productive, as those fabulous dragon's teeth; and being sown up and down, may chance to spring up armed men. And yet on the other hand, unless wariness be used, as good almost kill a man as kill a good book; who kills a man kills a reasonable creature, God's image; but he who destroys a good book, kills reason itself, kills the image of God, as it were in the eye. Many a man lives a burden to the earth; but a good book is the precious lifeblood of a master spirit, imbalmed and treasured up on purpose to a life beyond life."

—Milton's Speech for the License of Printing.

www.ingramcontent.com/pod-product-compliance
Lightning Source LLC
LaVergne TN
LVHW011147110826
845150LV00008B/2561
9781418191658